# DOUBLE OR QUITS
## Two Plays

Bryan Peppin

authorHOUSE®

AuthorHouse™
1663 Liberty Drive
Bloomington, IN 47403
www.authorhouse.com
Phone: 1-800-839-8640

These plays are entirely works of fiction. Any resemblance to the characters in
the plays to any person, living or dead, is unintentional and coincidental.

First published by AuthorHouse 12/14/2011

ISBN: 978-1-4678-8233-0 (sc)
ISBN: 978-1-4678-8234-7 (e)

Printed in the United States of America

Any people depicted in stock imagery provided by Thinkstock are models,
and such images are being used for illustrative purposes only.
Certain stock imagery © Thinkstock.

This book is printed on acid-free paper.

# DANIEL, PLEASE
## OR
# A DAY IN THE LIFE

**The Cast:**

**Paulsamy:** Fifty-one; corpulent, polished, cosmopolitan.

**Oliver**: Forty-two; cheeky, freaky, with a way.

**Sebastian**: Fifty-five; mousey, queasy, with another way.

**Yesuraj**: Fifty; flippant, light-headed, opinionated.

**Xavier**: Forty-five; headstrong, blinkered, blind.

**Anthony**: Fifty-seven; gross, coarse, ingratiating.

**Peon**: Fifty-five; dirty, greedy, inquisitive.

———————————

*The English Department of a suburban Madras college.*

*In a big, square room, twenty by twenty, six tables are arranged, two each to the opposite walls, and one on the far side. Closest to the entrance of the room is the bigger table of the Head of the Department. There are three other chairs opposite the HOD's table, and sundry others scattered in the room. The atmosphere exuded is one of satisfaction, inanity, ease.*

*In a far corner of the room is a dirty porcelain wash-basin. Next to it is a small, bare, wooden table, with a thermos on it. Around the thermos, visibly filthy, are cups and mugs— no saucers—which are even filthier.*

*Above the HOD's table is a medium-sized clock.*

*The Headship has not yet been decided officially, but everyone tacitly accepts that it is Sebastian's.*

*Each teaching session lasts 50 minutes, starting at 9.00 in the morning.*

———————————

# SCENE ONE

*It's nine-fifteen on Monday morning. Paulsamy and Oliver are sitting at their respective tables, which are adjacent to each other. Paulsamy is smoking, while Oliver is busy coaxing a beedi to life.*

**Paulsamy**: So the HOD's late again, as usual.

**Oliver**: Who? Who's the HOD?

**Paulsamy**: Who else? Come on, Oliver. Everyone knows Sebastian's the new HOD.

**Oliver**: Well, you know much more than I do. That's for sure.

**Paulsamy**: He got his orders on Friday... I think.

**Oliver**: Really? I didn't know.

**Paulsamy** (*stubbing out his cigarette*): He ought to have been here by now. On his first day, too.

**Oliver**: You know Sebastian. He can never change. It's too late for that. And talking about late-coming, just look at the time. It's way past nine. And ...

*Sebastian comes bustling in with a "**Good morning, gentlemen**", and, without any hesitation, walks to the HOD's table.*

**Oliver**: Enter the HOD.

*A brief silence follows as Sebastian settles himself in. Paulsamy and Oliver look on, both visibly amused.*

**Sebastian**: Where are the others? Anyone absent? Anything happening?

**Oliver**: Gone to class. No. Nothing really.

**Sebastian**: Nothing really begets nothing, son.

**Oliver**: I know that, nuncle.

**Sebastian**: Bastard.

**Oliver**: OK, Daddy.

**Sebastian**: When do I have a class?

**Oliver**: Not today. The last hour for the second M.A. class is put down for you, but that looks after itself.

**Sebastian**: Thank God! I'm too tired today. Bloody wheezing kept me awake all night. I'm not in the mood for any class. If there were one, I'd cancel it, anyway.

**Oliver**: I know.

**Paulsamy**: Hey, come on, Olive! Don't be too hard on him.

And haven't you got anything better to say than "I know" and "I don't know"?

**Oliver**: I know I say what I mean.

**Sebastian**: Bastard.

*A faint smile spreads over Sebastian's face.*

**Sebastian**: You know and do not know …

**Oliver** (*butting in*): That the wheel turns, Daddy?

**Sebastian**: Damn you, Oliver.

Paul, any news from the Principal? He said he had something for me. Don't know what. Wonder what it is.

**Paulsamy**: I thought it was all settled.

*A student, only his head inside the room, asks: "**Has Mr. Xavier come today, Sir?**" This is answered with an abrupt "**Yes**", by Oliver, and the room returns to normal.*

**Paulsamy**: You got your orders on Friday, didn't you, Sebastian?

**Sebastian**: That's just it. When I went to the Principal's room on Friday, he told me to take over the Department. The words were simply oral instructions.

**Paulsamy and Oliver**: What?

**Sebastian**: That's what they are. No written appointment. No indication that one was on its way. Nothing.

**Oliver**: Nothing begets nothing, Daddy.

**Sebastian**: Oh ... Fuck you and Shakespeare!

**Oliver**: He gives you your daily bread, Daddy. Pity the poor manunkindnot.

**Sebastian**: Be serious for once, Oliver.

**Oliver**: As I've heard said, many times over: "I'm normal when I'm mad."

**Paulsamy**: OK. OK. Sebastian, you really didn't get a regular appointment letter?

**Sebastian**: Of course I didn't. I don't know what's going on. And something tells me there's mischief about. I just have that feeling.

**Paulsamy**: Oh! Forget it, Sebastian. It's all settled.

*Oliver lights up another beedi and coughs deliberately.*

**Sebastian** (*to Oliver*): Can't you smoke regular cigarettes? Not all your study of literature has raised your level. And why are you smirking, anyway?

**Oliver**: First things first. Beedis have nothing to do with culture or civilization or level. It's simply a question of taste—personal taste. I like them, I smoke them. After all, one man's Mede is another man's Persian! So cut that crap out.

As to my smirking, that's another question. I was just looking at my ring and thinking: "That's a pearl that was an oyster." Have you ever had such thoughts? Have you ever been pried open and robbed of your preciousness— that part of you that took so long in the making, and which managed, finally, to turn into a thing of beauty?

For just how long you can afford to say: "My time has not yet come," I really don't know.

But remember this: the days of miracles have vanished forever.

*The bell rings—auspiciously—announcing the end of the first session. Oliver instinctively claps his hands to his ears and, with disgust, a low, whispered: "**Fucks**" escapes from his lips.*

*After the bell stops ringing, Oliver stands up.*

**Oliver**: (*declaiming*): Here comes the mob!

---

# SCENE TWO

*Half an hour later. The room still sports some slivers of smoke. Oliver is half-way through a cigarette, for a change. He is pensively thinking about nothing. There is no one else in the room at the moment; a deep sigh escapes from him.*

*His face mirrors wryness as Sebastian comes in with a bundle of papers.*

**Oliver**: What's new, pussycat?

*Sebastian puts the papers down, tries to shuffle them into some kind of order, looks around furtively, and then adopts a decidedly low, confidential tone.*

**Sebastian**: These bastards are really at it, Oliver. I didn't know they could stoop so low. They've reported to the authorities that because I'm on medical leave so often, I won't be able to do justice to the Department. And those people are only too ready to listen to them.

What's even worse, they've spread a canard that I've denigrated their religion. Tell me honestly, Oliver, do you think that I, a Christian myself, could ever have done such a thing?

**Oliver**: Daddy, haven't I always told you to keep your mouth shut? You talk too much. And to the wrong people most of the time.

7

I've told you again and again that these bastards are fanatics. What's worse, they're hypocritical fanatics.

I don't know if it's because we're the only Catholics in the Department—the only two in the College, for that matter—that we seem to confide in each other. But that does seem to be one of the strongest ties that we have.

Have you not noticed the closed sessions, the hushed conversations, and the embarrassed looks that we encounter, when we butt in? Of course, something's going on! And I have kept warning you. They've tried to hide it, but it's apparent in everything they say and do.

Surely some revelation is at hand.

**Sebastian**: But what have I done? Do I deserve this? Is there any rationale in their bias? I've been in this place for thirty years, and only of late have I felt alien. All my sweat and blood has been given to this dump, and when I reach the top, the bastards want to pull me down.

**Oliver**: Hey, Hey! Take it easy. You've simply not taken note of the fact that religion is thicker—and stickier—than blood.

**Sebastian**: But why this sudden change?

**Oliver**: "I see," said the blind man.

**Sebastian**: Come on, Oliver. If this happens to me, it will certainly happen to you, sooner or later.

**Oliver**: Even if it does seem smug, Daddy, I've steeled myself to that possibility. And anyway, who knows, this cuckoo may fly.

**Sebastian**: But son, if this is supposed to be a policy decision, it should have been implemented right from the beginning.

**Oliver**: That would have been disastrous, Daddy.

Can't you see that more than half the fellows in this College are here simply because they were born into the right denomination?

Remember what the students told the Principal when he called a meeting to discuss Department matters? What did he do? Nothing! He got to the truth, but it hurt him—personally, too—to learn that his men were all balls. The difference is so great, it's embarrassing.

Your time—and even mine—was different. They wanted the place to have the best; of what was available, at least. We may not be really "there", but the other fuckers are a far way off.

But now? Who cares for quality?

The whole damned country runs on mediocrity—from top to bottom.

Any bugger with brains or enterprise or both has to get out. Unfortunately, we're still here. And destined to stay, forever and forever, amen.

So forget about justice, reason, horse-sense, what-not! It's no longer a brave new world. But you can still take heart: when the mind is free, nothing else matters.

Readiness is all.

**Sebastian**: I suppose you're right.

But why did they choose me to be the scapegoat? I've done nothing to justify their making me a sacrificial victim.

I'm known as a good teacher all over Madras, and perhaps all over India too. Some of my students occupy high positions. Why shouldn't I? After all, this isn't Parnassus. And surely I deserve this after slogging for so long.

Why me, why me?

*The Department peon shuffles in, goes to the wash-basin, rinses the cups, then the thermos, and looks in the direction of Sebastian.*

**Peon**: Sir, tea?

**Sebastian**: No!

**Peon**: Hot tea, Sir?

**Sebastian** (*testily*): I said "No"!

*As the peon goes out, the bell rings again, signaling the end of the second session. There is an immediate bustle outside the room, typical of unruly college behavior.*

**Sebastian**: So you have a class now, eh? Well, I'll see you after that. And don't breathe a word to anyone, OK?

---

# SCENE THREE

*Twenty minutes later. The peon is pouring tea into the cups.*

*Xavier, Anthony, and Yesuraj are huddled together in close conference. They speak in stealthy undertones.*

*Xavier has something of an English accent about him, but affectation somehow spoils the effect. Anthony's speech reminds one of a person gulping and gasping at the same time, while Yesuraj speaks with the sing-song characteristic of a sizable majority of the men from the south-west of the country.*

**Yesuraj**: You know what? The fellows have finally downed it. Dirty rascals. Bloody rotten scoundrels. Because they have strength in numbers, they do what they want. They don't care about other people and what they feel and all that.

**Xavier**: You're right, Yesu. There's only jungle law in this country.

**Anthony**: Suppose if it had been the other way round, I say. There would have been hell to play.

**Xavier**: I don't think that kind of thing will ever happen, Anthony Sir. But if it's happened there already, it could happen here anytime. Who knows, some other religious edifice may be the next target.

And they're also saying that some should go to Pakistan and others to England. There's no safety here any more. Might is now right. The law of the jungle has taken over.

**Yesuraj**: And they continue to interfere in internal matters and all that. Look at our College. It's meant for us, isn't it? Why can't we have our own choice when it comes to Principal-ship? Or Head-ship? Why should we always be magnanimous? The other institutions aren't.

Why, even on days which are important religious festivals, classes are conducted in some of them. So why should we alone be fair? They don't care about justice and all that. We should also be the same.

Why, even in our Department, Anthony Sir should have been made the Head. Who knows, he may still take over. No written order has been given to Mr. Sebastian yet.

**Anthony**: No, I say. I don't aspire for the post. I have only a year left.

**Xavier**: So what, Anthony Sir? It's our College. We must get what we want. If someone else gets the job, then what's the use of our working here? Look at the other colleges in the city. They're all stacked with the right men. And when it comes to position, they don't hesitate to overlook seniority, or talent, or other considerations. So why should we?

**Yesuraj**: Correct, Xavier. I hope things will work out that way here also, because they ought to know where they stand and all that. We must pay them back in their own coin, in whatever way we can. To hell with fair play.

*Sebastian comes into the room. The other three exchange silent, meaningful looks.*

**Anthony**: Good morning, Mr. Sebastian. I didn't see you this morning. I had two consecutive classes. How are you? Any news? Should I offer you my congratulations?

**Sebastian**: 'Morning to all of you. No, no, Anthony. Congratulations? For what? I don't know anything for sure.

*Xavier and Yesuraj exchange glances again. A scowl flits across Xavier's face.*

**Anthony**: But, Sir! I thought everything was over. You're the senior-most amongst us. Why do they need to look around? You're the logical choice, surely.

**Sebastian**: Thank you for saying that, Anthony. I'm happy that at least some of my friends think that way. But I can hardly presume to know their minds. And all this delay is getting to me. But it is some comfort to know that I still have some real friends and well-wishers.

**Yesuraj**: What do you mean by that, Sir?

**Sebastian**: Don't get me wrong, Yesu. I didn't mean anyone in particular. But the very air smells of machination. God knows I've done my bit for the College. As much as anyone else. But …

**Anthony**: Forget it, Sir. Personally, I would be very happy to have you as HOD.

**Sebastian**: Thanks, Anthony. Thank you very much. I really mean it when I say I appreciate those sentiments.

**Anthony**: It's all right, Mr. Sebastian. Forget it. Would you like some tea?

*The bell rings once more, monotonously, announcing the end of the third session.*

# SCENE FOUR

*Twenty- five minutes later. The room is un-occupied at the moment, and remains so for about thirty seconds. A shuffling of feet is heard, immediately followed by sounds of laughter. One laugh is tentative and forced, while the other is coarse and raucous.*

*Anthony, a dark-red rexine carry-bag under his arm, and Xavier, blowing cigarette smoke, stroll in. Anthony is still laughing.*

**Xavier**: So what did he say, finally?

**Anthony**: About what?

**Xavier**: The rendezvous.

**Anthony**: Oh yes, I forgot. Yes. He told me all about his adventures last night. It seems he was waiting at the Chola bus-stop. He had his scooter parked some distance away, so he walked to the bus-stop. He said he waited about twenty minutes for a prospective catch. He nearly lost an opportunity because of his impatience. But finally she arrived, I say. There had been a heavy drizzle at that time, and that made it easier for him. He nudged his way closer to her—and very carefully too—and then began the assault.

**Xavier**: You mean Yesu actually did all that last night?

**Anthony**: Yes, I say. The usual method. He told me himself. He said it was about nine-fifteen and that he waited for about ten minutes to open up a conversation. Of course, he kept glancing at her meaningfully—you know Yesu's way—and she didn't turn away. So he asked her if he could drop her home. After some reluctance on her part, she agreed. It started raining heavily, it seems. They had to take refuge in a cheap restaurant. But that gave Yesu the chance to find out things about her. When the rain subsided they pushed off. And Yesu told me that she was clinging on to him so tightly that he got excited. Anyway, it was about ten-thirty when he dropped her off at Kotturpuram. She promised to meet him today, and that's why he's still so bubbly.

**Xavier**: Yes. I saw that. Catch Yesu offering anyone a cup of tea in ordinary circumstances. But what I don't understand, Anthony Sir, is how women can bear the sight of the fellow. I don't think half of what he tells us is true.

**Anthony**: I suppose every dog will have its day.

**Xavier**: If it's as he says, he's a lucky dog. Didn't he say he'd be joining us in a few minutes?

**Anthony**: Yes, he did. He had some urgent business. That's why he took his scooter. He has to come back; he's got a class next hour.

**Xavier**: General English, or Literature?

**Anthony**: General. Science "A" batch, I think.

**Xavier**: Then he will come back. That batch has its class just above the Principal's office.

*Yesuraj comes in swaggering, throws his keys on the table, sits, puts a cigarette to his lips, and lights it carefully. His hands are cupped around the flame, and his beady eyes are glued there, too.*

**Xavier**: So, Yesu, another conquest, eh?

**Yesuraj**: What is it, I say? Nothing new. I've been doing this for decades. One day I'm lucky, one day I'm not. Yesterday I was lucky. Today may be better. Tomorrow, who knows?

**Xavier**: But tell me, Yesu. Why do women run after you so much?

**Yesuraj**: As if you don't know, I say. Charm, for sure. I suppose that comes to me naturally. But the thing that really turns them on is something quite different. When they learn that I'm an English lecturer (*pronounced "lecherer"*), that seals it. Every time it works, I say. Then the usual games and all that.

**Anthony**: Suppose if your wife finds out about your tricks, Yesu.

**Yesuraj**: Damn it. Wife is for home. Even if she finds out, what can she do? Anyway, I don't care. This is my life.

**Xavier**: You mean horsing around?

**Yesuraj**: Whatever around. I can't stay at home in the evenings, that's all.

*Sebastian comes into the room and the banter stops. Yesuraj raises a hand in mock greeting. Sebastian returns it with a wave, and sits down at his table. With elbows on the table and his face in the palms of his hands, he looks at them.*

**Sebastian**: How many minutes more for the bell?

**Anthony**: Five minutes, Sir. Eight, to be exact. Why?

**Sebastian**: Nothing really. I was just wondering where everyone was. I haven't seen Paulsamy and Oliver since this morning. And what's happened to the peon? That fellow is never here. I don't know what to do.

**Xavier**: You must be firm, Sir. Tell the Principal about it. And follow it up.

**Sebastian**: How many times do I have to make complaints? That man asks me to put it in writing. What authority do I have for that? I'm supposed to be the HOD, but even that hasn't been confirmed in writing. So how can I put anything down in black and white? Who knows? They may even use the letter against me.

I don't know what this College is heading towards. But, to my mind, it doesn't seem to be going anywhere. And it just doesn't seem to have any system, either; just the same old rigmarole, day after day after day.

*Yesuraj and Xavier, who have been listening intently to Sebastian all this time, exchange glances.*

*Paulsamy comes in, looking a little deflated. He hardly notices the other three in the room, and plonks into a chair opposite Sebastian's table. The other three are seated behind Paulsamy, and he knows it. He takes out his cigarette packet, lights up, inhales deeply, and almost caresses the smoke as he blows it softly out.*

**Paulsamy**: Hell! Two hours at a stretch is getting horrible these days.

**Sebastian**: Yes, I know.

**Paulsamy**: I don't know if I can take it much longer.

**Sebastian**: I understand what you mean, Paul. Age has a subtle, sly way of catching up with one.

**Paulsamy**: Whew! I'm pooped. And hungry. What's for lunch today?

**Sebastian**: I don't know. I think it's a fishy day. Oliver's sent for the grub.

**Paulsamy**: Where is he? He had only one class today—in the third hour.

*The bell goes off again, signaling the end of the fourth session. Oliver comes in, takes up Paulsamy's cigarette packet, takes a cigarette out very carefully, lights up, and sits down next to Paulsamy. He, too, avoids the other three behind them.*

*The bell stops ringing. Anthony, Yesuraj, and Xavier stream out, books in hand. After they have quitted the room, Sebastian mutters to himself, almost in a soft incantation.*

**Oliver**: What?

**Sebastian** (*turning his face to the door*): Go, sad, erring fools.

---

# SCENE FIVE

*Five minutes later. Paulsamy and Oliver are smoking. Sebastian is peering at some papers and, at the same time, making notes. Oliver gets up from his chair, walks to the far window, takes a final puff, and pitches the cigarette butt through the window grille. Paulsamy leaves his seat, takes one opposite Sebastian's table, and draws out yet another cigarette even before finishing the earlier one. He takes a puff, throws the butt to the floor, crushes it, and lights up afresh.*

*Oliver paces the room in very deliberate strides, and continues the exercise, back and forth.*

**Sebastian**: What the hell are you doing, Oliver?

**Oliver**: Just getting ready for lunch.

**Sebastian**: Haven't you got anything better to do?

**Oliver**: No, but I do have something to say.

**Sebastian**: What's that?

**Oliver**: Well, I've been thinking about this for a long time. I've served in this place for twenty years and I think I've finally become useless.

**Paulsamy**: How's that?

**Sebastian**: Yes, tell us.

*Oliver sits down and begins, in all seriousness.*

*All through the rest of the scene Paulsamy and Oliver smoke, oblivious of, and seemingly uncaring for, Sebastian's respiratory condition.*

**Oliver**: Well, I can only speak about myself. What you infer doesn't concern me.

What I'm getting at is that the system has crippled me. I now know less than I did fifteen years ago. Yet I believe that I've improved over the years. Experience is a wonderful thing, but if the routine is repeated over and over again, the experience counts for nothing.

Tell me honestly, if all the teachers of English in all the city colleges were to take their M.A. exams again—on the hop, mind you—how many would pass all papers? My guess is, less than ten percent.

You see, when some of us did take our degrees, we managed to pass. But at that time we were at least conversant with literature through the ages. As soon as we began to teach, certain authors or ages were allotted to us. If we were lucky, or the HOD's blue-eyed boys, we got to choose our subjects. And then, we soon became straight-jacketed. And all our visions dimmed, and our horizons stopped expanding. And when that happens, worse things must ensue.

**Paulsamy**: For whom?

**Oliver**: For the learners, of course. Year by year we sink deeper and deeper into one particular groove. And if re-arrangement is contemplated, it is looked upon with indignation.

But unless we change minute by minute, we cannot hope to be better than hollow men. Quartz contentment takes over, Lotos-land stupor follows, and this leads to atrophy and intellectual death.

And so, I'm now quite useless.

**Sebastian**: Perhaps you're being too harsh, Oliver. I do agree that many people in the profession hardly deserve the name of "teacher". Chaudhari got his percentages wrong when he wrote about civil servants and university lecturers. I think closer to ninety percent of all the college teachers in this country would make good shop-keepers.

But what's to be done? India is churning out hundreds of thousands of degree holders who go to face desolate reality armed with a worthless piece of paper.

There must be hundreds of bus-conductors with post-graduate degrees. I've come across an application from a qualified medical practitioner seeking employment as a language teacher!

I've seen excellent teacher material being turned away for want a paper degree. And this when the man in question could not only hold his own, but outshine, most scholars, here in India, or anywhere in the world.

But you cannot change the system. It's too firmly entrenched. And no one really wants it changed. Not even the students.

What would happen to all the manipulation now possible, if things were cleaned up? No, no, that would never do!

**Oliver**: Who said the system cannot be broken? History is replete with examples of sudden, drastic change. Sometimes the new order is preceded by violence, but it doesn't have to be so.

**Paulsamy**: It's not that easy, Olive. Think of all the peoples' lives that would be disrupted if the system were changed.

Now, when a man joins a college as a lecturer, he is guaranteed an ever-increasing pension for the whole of his active life. All he needs is the minimum qualifications; and the right connections. And, in a college like ours, the right brand. No one really looks into the man's professional competence, no one bothers about his moral worth, or worthlessness, and no one cares a whit what damage he can do. And this laissez-faire attitude seeps into everything.

But, as Sebastian says, who cares a damn.

**Sebastian**: Yes, yes. The best lack all conviction.

**Oliver** I know.

*Paulsamy shifts his position in his chair and Oliver gets up to pace the room again.*

**Sebastian**: Do you think anyone can really teach literature?

**Paulsamy**: I don't think so.

**Oliver**: That's obvious, isn't it? But every person has a different notion regarding culture. And literature is only one branch of that. Just the other afternoon I was sitting in the library—the American one. Suddenly, incredibly, a man—well dressed and perfectly composed—farted loudly and long. All the people there stared at him; some sniggered. But the man went on reading, unperturbed. There's a culture-clash for you. The fellow probably didn't know such a thing is considered impolite in most societies.

**Sebastian**: You have a point there, Oliver.

You and I, and Paul, of course, have been to umpteen valuation camps. What do we see there? Old men ogling the ladies, younger men parading their idiocy, women—not ladies—slovenly dressed … the works. I have often sympathized with the students whose papers are corrected by such specimens.

And talking about correction: did you hear about the teacher who gave fifty-three marks in Paper IV of the M.A. exam? The second examiner awarded zero. When the paper went for the third valuation, it was marked zero again. What happened to the fellow who gave fifty-three? He was taken off the panel for two years. That's all. He should have been sacked!

**Paulsamy**: Yes, but that's history now.

**Oliver**: What can we do? What shall we ever do? Is that all we're going to ask, forever?

**Sebastian**: Forget it, Oliver. Let me tell you about this video program at the American Center. This woman was moderating a discussion on Anne Sexton. Clumsily dressed, she couldn't even hide a pair of ugly feet, marred further by soles with blackened cracks. I just couldn't help thinking to myself: "How can this woman have the audacity to speak about Anne Sexton?" My God!

*The peon comes in, busily, a huge tiffin-carrier in one hand, and a small jerry-can of water in the other. He puts the carrier on the table next to the wash-basin, bends down at Oliver's table, draws out four stainless-steel plates, and proceeds to rinse them.*

**Peon**: Lunch ready, Sir.

**Sebastian**: OK, OK, we're coming. You'll get your share, don't worry. But go first to the Principal's office and see if he has anything for me. Understand?

**Peon**: Yes, Sir.

*The peon leaves the room. Sebastian and Paulsamy and Oliver go over to the wash-basin, and go through the rituals*

23

*of washing their plates and their hands. They then sit down to lunch. Paulsamy opens up the tiffin-carrier and starts serving.*

**Oliver**: Why don't they get rid of all the courses that have no utility value?

**Sebastian**: You mean literature has no value, Oliver?

**Oliver**: Yes, something like that.

There are other core courses that need to be scrapped, too. Or, at least, they shouldn't be offered as they are right now. They can be replaced by more comprehensive courses— Life Sciences, or Physical Sciences, or Population Studies, and so on.

What an average student gets right now for all his efforts is a lot of useless—in the sense unusable—information. And all this is never put to use in his everyday life. So what need for all this crap?

**Paulsamy**: Finish off with this first, Olive (*pointing to the food*).

**Sebastian**: Yes, one thing at a time.

**Oliver**: All right. But I haven't finished.

*All three get down to the business of eating. It doesn't present a pleasing picture; there is something somber about their deliberations.*

**Oliver**: Not bad. The fish is quite tasty today.

**Paulsamy**: Yes.

*Fresh helpings are served out and Oliver is the first to finish.*

*He rinses his plate, takes a cigarette from Paulsamy, lights up, and sits down. He watches the others still eating.*

**Oliver**: Well? Shall I continue?

**Sebastian**: If you must. But what's happened to the peon?

**Paulsamy**: Don't worry, he'll be back.

**Oliver**: A little earlier Sebastian asked if literature can be taught at all. I think we should ask if we ought to teach literature in the first place. And my answer is a firm "No". Or if they—different literatures, I mean—cannot be dispensed with, these special courses should be made so financially prohibitive that only those who really want to should join them.

Let's have more doctors and engineers and computer experts.

But let's make the study of literature exclusive. It is, after all, not everyone's cup of tea. And what we now get as student material is just the rejects and castaways from the other courses. What motivation can such fellows have? And do such types ever want to—if that is possible—comprehend Chaucer, or Blake, or Yeats, or Eliot, or Stevens? When they do get their degrees, they're sometimes worse off than when they started; and practically fit for nothing.

*Sebastian finishes his lunch, cleans up, and sits down. Paulsamy then does the same, and ends up with a cigarette.*

**Sebastian**: But what the hell will happen to all of us?

**Oliver**: Well, for those of us who are flexible enough, we can be transformed into language teachers. God knows we need a lot of them; and certainly many, many more with better communication skills. That's what we lack most and need so very much. Students now pass their English examinations without knowing how to compose a single line. Many of the teachers are not much better, anyway. So if we stay the way we are, we're doomed.

**Sebastian**: But we simply cannot do away with literature, Oliver.

**Paulsamy**: Yes, I'm sure Sebastian's right.

**Oliver**: To hell with the subject, as it is now taught. Do you want to know why I think it should go?

I'll tell you, anyway.

I remember teaching a group of M. Phil. students—all women, at that—the poetry of Adrienne Rich. When it came to the crunch, all of them backed out, and I was the only die-hard feminist in the class. What capped it all was a comment from one of them. "Sir," she said, "Don't teach us things like that. We'll get into trouble with our husbands!" So **Aunt Jennifer's Tigers** are only phantoms; and they will remain so, over here, unchanging forever.

*The peon arrives, hot and sweaty.*

**Sebastian**: Anything?

**Peon**: No, Sir. Nothing, Sir.

**Sebastian**: What did he say?

**Peon**: Nothing, Sir.

*The bell goes off again. This time it's a long-drawn-out ringing, signaling the end of the day.*

*The men in the room seem calm, but disquiet and despair wrack Sebastian's face. He looks more and more despondent.*

*The peon sits down to his food, as the sounds of release from the class-rooms flood the room.*

*Anthony, Yesuraj, and Xavier file in. They dump their books on their respective tables and make preparations for immediate departure. When all of them see that they are ready, they move to the door. Their words are almost hurled back at those remaining.*

**Anthony**: Goodnight.

**Yesuraj**: Goodnight.

**Xavier**: Goodnight.

**Sebastian**: Goodnight. Gentlemen, goodnight.

*Sebastian heaves a tremendous sigh. Paulsamy and Oliver can do nothing but watch.*

**Sebastian**: Well, it's over, finished. And nothing again. Tomorrow, perhaps.

*Sebastian shrugs his shoulders.*

*Paulsamy and Oliver look at the floor.*

*The peon continues eating.*

**Sebastian**: We meet again tomorrow. Until then, so long. Good night.

*As Sebastian, Paulsamy, and Oliver leave the room, the peon looks up from his gorging and smiles awkwardly.*

---

# CURTAIN

# UPSIDE DOWN
## OR
# A LIFE IN A DAY

# UPSIDE DOWN
# OR
# A LIFE IN A DAY

**The Cast:**

**Oliver**: Thirty-five.

**Deb**: Thirty-three; Oliver's wife.

**Ruku**: Around sixty; their "ayah".

**Srini**: Forty; Oliver's friend and colleague.

**Abdu**: Forty-eight; another colleague.

**Ebby**: Forty-five; yet another colleague.

**Ozzie**: Six; Oliver's second son.

**Junior**: Ten; Oliver's first son.

**Saleem**: Eleven; Junior's friend.

---

**Oliver's Mother.**

**Lady in Sari.**

**"Child" Oliver.**

---

**Vikram**: Around ten; "Boy" Oliver's friend.

**Vikram's Mother.**

(Another) **Lady in Sari.**

**"Boy" Oliver.**

---

**TEN YEARS LATER**

**Shirin**: Thirty-three.

**Fauzia**: Four; Shirin's second daughter.

**Farida**: Six; Shirin's first daughter.

**Mahmood**: Thirty-six; Shirin's husband.

**Mary**: Around forty-five; their maid.

---

**Manager of the Bar.**

**Bearer.**

*The action of the first three* **Acts** *of the play takes place in the home of Oliver and Deb.*

*The fourth* **Act** *takes place in the home of Mahmood and Shirin, ten years later.*

*The fifth* **Act** *takes place in the Bar of a Madras hotel.*

*Since some of the scenes-within-scenes are* **flashback-memories***, Oliver is found seated, appropriately, up front of the set (closer to a corner, preferably) in these. The spotlight focuses on him as the rest of the scene fades away, resulting in the real presentation of the flashback-memory. The process is reversed when the flashback-memory is completed.*

*The home of Oliver and Deb.*

*During the* **First Act***, the action is concentrated in the living room. It is a spacious, rectangular room, fifteen by twenty. The distemper on the walls is a pale lilac. In the middle of the rear wall is a door leading to the dining room. A flowered curtain, not long enough, shields the inside view. The side walls boast broad windows of steel grille, painted gray. No curtains adorn the windows; there isn't one for the front door, too.*

*There are two three-sitter settees, one to each of the side walls. Four cane chairs flank the settees, two to each side, separated from them by cane teapoys. In the center of the room, on the shining, gray-mosaic floor, is a round, mahogany table with flower-vase and ash-tray. On both sides of the door leading to the dining room are built-up shelves, which house a television and a video on one side, and a music system on the other. Some of the upper shelves are filled with art objects, and everything is presided over by a large portrait of the Christ, just above the connecting door.*

# ACT ONE

## Scene One

*The music coming out of the system, a little too loud, is of "country" origin. Just as the next piece begins, Oliver comes into the room carrying an ash-tray. He is wearing jeans, a T-shirt, and slippers. He glances at the oval time-piece on the right wall; it shows eleven forty-five.*

*Oliver joins in with the music. The song now playing is Dolly Parton's version of **I Wanna Go Home**, as he identifies it—**Detroit City**, actually. Oliver's singing is not too bad; in fact, it is something he is quite proud of. His singing gets louder. There is a definite hint of emotion in his voice when the chorus comes along. He checks himself, lights up a cigarette, and looks around the room with satisfaction. He then goes to the front door and looks out, happily, yet with a peering gaze.*

*Deb comes in through the connecting door. She is elegantly dressed in a bright, cotton frock and baby-doll-heeled shoes. There is a ripe maturity in her demeanor, the kind a woman has when she is confident—of everything.*

**Deb**: I thought your friends were coming over at eleven-thirty.

*Oliver turns around to take in the picture she presents. There is obvious pleasure in his face.*

**Oliver**: Yeah. They'll be here soon.

*He stubs out his cigarette and catches Deb up in a bear-hug.*

**Oliver**: C'mon, let's dance.

*Deb struggles, but cannot escape. She relents and falls into step.*

**Deb**: Someone will be watching, Ollie.

**Oliver**: So what? You're my wife. This is our home.

**Deb**: For just a little while more, Ol.

**Oliver**: So what? It's still ours. Let's make the most of it. Who knows what will happen in the future?

*There is a pause in the music, and Deb breaks free. Then, putting her hands on Oliver's chest, she looks at him lovingly.*

**Deb**: Don't worry, love. It will be all right.

*Oliver presses a kiss on her forehead and sits down. Deb takes her place next to him. She takes his hand in both of hers, and he grips hard.*

**Deb**: I'm going to Mel's place for some time, Ol.

**Oliver**: OK. But what about the boys? Where are they?

**Deb**: You know. They'll be back. Let them be. They've only got a few days left.

**Oliver**: Oh, all right. Have you given the old lady her instructions?

**Deb**: Yes. Anyway, let's call her and see if she's got it right.

*Looking in the direction of the kitchen, she calls out:*

**Deb**: Ruku; Ruku the cuckoo!

*From way behind comes a voice, obviously the ayah's.*

**Ruku**: Ace, ace, mees-ma. You calling me, missy? One nimit, ma; I put off gas an' come.

*Deb stands up, waiting for the ayah. She glances at the time-piece.*

*Ruku, the ayah, comes shuffling in. She is wearing a not-too-clean sari, and has a kitchen towel over her shoulder. She is dark-complexioned and plump, with straggly, gray-white hair tied up behind her head. Her hands bear testimony of cooking, and she looks hot and tired. Yet she has the contented look of a robust sixty-year-old, happy with her station in life.*

**Ruku**: Ace, mees-ma. Wot you call me fo'?

**Deb**: Bawa wants to know if everything is ready.

**Ruku**: Wot, ma. Still time is there. All be ready by one 'clock. O'ny little frying more. But all tip-top; first class.

**Oliver**: What have you made for us today, ma?

**Ruku**: Wot you said, Bawa. Fried rice, chicken vindaloo, cutlets, 'tato mash, an' onion an' 'mato salad. I make ornery rice too, Saar. Missy got thick curd in fridge. She also making ice-cream. Wot more you need, Bawa?

**Oliver**: What about the scramble, ma? They'll want it for their drinks.

**Ruku**: Yes, Saar. I make it now. Mus' be nice an' 'ot, no? Then o'ly good taste.

35

**Deb** (*laughing*): Don't worry, Ruku. Bawa'll keep your share.

**Ruku**: T'anks, missy. I no drink here. Take 'ome; 'ave in the night. Then o'ly I get good sleep.

**Deb**: OK, ayah. Thank you.

*Ruku goes through the connecting door.*

**Deb**: Right, Ol. I'll be back in an hour or so. And don't go too fast. We have to go out this evening, remember?

**Oliver**: OK, love. Come back soon.

*Deb goes out through the front door with a wave. Oliver walks up to the music system, chooses another LP, and replaces the old one. He lights up a cigarette and sits down, but immediately returns to the system to adjust the volume. As soon as he is satisfied, he returns to his chair. He gives himself to the mood and, in his pensiveness, doesn't seem to need any company.*

## Scene Two

*The same room.*

*Oliver is still sitting in the same chair, looking at the jacket of the LP. When the song is over, he gets up and goes into the dining room. He returns with a large glass of beer. He takes a pull and looks around the room. His eyes fix on the center-table and, remembering something, he goes back to the dining room. This time he returns with an ice pail and a tray with six glass tumblers on it. He puts the tray on the center-table, and the pail on the floor, beside it. He then takes another long swig, puts his glass on the teapoy, and lights up another cigarette. Once again he joins in with the song, but this time in an undertone.*

*He goes to the front door, pitches the cigarette into the yard and looks around. His face beams as he sees Abdu, Ebby, and Srini approaching.*

**Oliver**: At last. What kept you?

**Srini** (*pointing to Ebby*): This guy. He wanted to wait for 52G. We waited till 11.10 and then forced him into another bus. Are we very late?

**Oliver**: No, not at all. Welcome. Come on in. And forget that: you can keep your shoes on. Oh! Come on, Sir. It's all right.

**Abdu**: Thanks, Oliver. Wow! What have we here?

**Oliver**: Nothing unusual. Just what you would expect.

*The men sit down, and Abdu and Srini light up cigarettes. Oliver pushes the ash-tray towards them.*

**Ebby**: And where is Mrs. Oliver?

**Oliver**: She's gone to see a friend, here in the colony. Should be back in an hour or so.

**Abdu**: That's good … Well …

**Oliver**: Shall we start? What'll you have? Beer, to start with?

**Srini**: OK. What else have you got?

**Oliver**: Whiskey … And rum, for anyone who wants to join me. Give me a minute, OK?

*Oliver goes to the dining room.*

*The men look around, and Abdu notices Oliver's glass on the teapoy. Then he remembers something.*

**Abdu**: Oliver, bring something for the hot stuff. We brought some.

*Oliver returns with three beer-filled glasses on a tray, with an empty stainless-steel bowl on it too. He offers the beers to the others, and gives the bowl to Abdu, who empties the packet's contents into it.*

**Abdu**: Cheers.

**All**: Cheers.

**Ebby**: And let's wish Oliver and his family all the best.

*All of them take long pulls at their beers, and Abdu and Srini echo Ebby's sentiments.*

**Abdu**: Wow! That's good. Really chilled. Wonderful, wonderful.

**Srini**: So, Oliver, everything fixed?

**Oliver**: Yes, I suppose so. It's gonna take some time to adjust.

**Srini**: Don't worry, you'll make good.

**Oliver**: Yeah, thanks. I hope so.

*The LP clicks off and Oliver goes to turn off the system. The others munch away, and Oliver joins them.*

**Ebby**: So what are your plans, Oliver?

**Oliver**: Well, I'll be staying with my sister for a month or so. Hope it won't be any longer. I'll have to look around for a job. And settle the boys in school. If all goes well, my wife won't have to work. I'm not particular about the kind of job I get there, by the way. I'm fed up with teaching. What I'd really like to do is hit the road.

**Abdu**: You want to scour the country for girls, eh?

**Oliver**: No, not that, really. I'm past that … I think.

**Ebby**: Ho, ho, ho.

**Srini**: No one gets past that, Oliver. Remember the last escapade? Hell, that was something, wasn't it?

*All of them laugh heartily. Ebby looks around. When he's sure there is no one listening in, he relaxes.*

**Ebby**: C'mon Oliver. Don't tell me you're through with the girls. No one gets enough; even if there are plenty.

**Srini**: Yeah. Women and booze—that's the life.

**Abdu**: And when they're free, or cheap, one can go on and on and on.

**Oliver**: Well, yeah, I suppose that's the way with everyone. But somehow or other, I've never felt free with the girls. What I mean is that I don't know how to make the first move. But once contact is established, it's easy. And anyway, I'm not too interested in knowing every woman in town.

**Abdu**: But wouldn't you like to? I wouldn't mind, I'm sure. God knows I've had my share and more. But that hasn't

39

slaked anything. It's come to a stage when I'm not too choosy about my women.

**Srini**: Perhaps age has something to do with choice, Sir. At twenty-five you could afford to pick and choose. But at fifty, one must take what one gets.

**Abdu**: No, no. I'm not so hard up. But what I mean is that most women will do for me now.

**Srini**: Including maids?

**Ebby**: Tell me honestly, is there any man in the world who hasn't had a go with that sort; or at least hasn't had serious thoughts about it? It's only natural, I say, especially when one is young and fiery.

**Srini**: Yeah, Ebby, I know you're a master there. But you've forgotten the old and the lecherous. I don't know about the others … and modesty forbids …

*Ozzie, Oliver's younger son, comes running through the front door. He stops and looks at the assembly curiously, but keeps his distance.*

**Oliver**: Come here, son. Say "Good morning" to my friends.

*Ozzie just stands there.*

**Oliver**: Say "Good morning", Ozzie.

*Ozzie continues to stand, silent. An unpleasant expression flits across Oliver's face. One of the men breaks the silence.*

**Ebby**: It's OK, Oliver. Ozzie's not in a good mood. Come here, son. Take some of this.

*Ebby offers Ozzie some hot stuff, which he grabs with both hands, and disappears into the dining room. Oliver follows him, but is soon back, with a bottle of whiskey, and another of rum. He begins to serve.*

**Oliver**: Please don't mind me if I'm a little quiet. I'm in a somewhat reflective mood at the moment. And please help yourselves. There's more inside.

**Abdu, Ebby, and Srini** (*all together*): OK. Yeah. Don't worry, we understand.

*Ozzie rushes into the room, grabs a hand-full of hot stuff and, with a hurried "Good morning" and grin, goes out the front door.*

*A puzzled look comes across Oliver. He takes a deep pull at his rum and leans back in his chair. Taking a cigarette from the center-table, he lights up and relaxes once more. There is a distant look on his face.*

*While the others engage themselves in small talk, Oliver lapses back.*

### Flashback-memory:

> *A shabby-genteel living room. Photographs of family on the walls. Two-seater cane sofa and two arm-chairs, all painted dark green. A radio in one corner.*
>
> *Oliver's mother and Lady in Sari in conversation. "Child" Oliver comes into the room.*
>
> **Oliver's Mother**: This is my son, Oliver. Oliver, say "Good evening" to this Aunty.
>
> *"Child" Oliver stays put, silent.*

**Oliver's Mother**: Say "Good evening", Oliver.

*"Child" Oliver refuses to respond, but remains where he is.*

**Lady in Sari**: It's OK, Ma'am. Well, I'd better be going. See you in school tomorrow.

**Oliver's Mother**: OK. 'Bye.

*Oliver's Mother sees the lady out of the room and returns to "Child" Oliver. He is still standing there, in the same place.*

**Oliver's Mother**: You're a bad boy, Oliver. Why didn't you say "Good evening" to that Aunty?

**"Child" Oliver**: She's not my Aunty. You only told me that only ayahs wear saris.

**Ruku**: Bawa, Bawa.

*Oliver is jerked back to the present with a call from the maid.*

**Oliver**: Yes? Oh, yes, I forgot. Thank you, ma. Gentlemen, scrambled eggs!

**Ruku**: You want anyt'ing else, Bawa?

**Oliver**: No, ma, no. This will do for the present.

*Ruku shuffles off back to the kitchen.*

**Oliver**: Why are you all going so slow? Come on, fill up. I told you: there's lots more.

*Oliver refills all the glasses and sits down.*

**Srini**: Ebby, do you really think all men are the same? I mean, are they prone to temptation on even the slightest premise?

**Ebby**: Er, generally, yes. Definitely yes. A man who isn't interested in a skirt isn't a man ... in my line of thinking.

**Srini**: But that damns us all as lascivious, lewd animals.

**Ebby**: Which is what we are. But pretend not to be.

**Oliver**: I tend to agree.

**Abdu**: You too, Oliver?

**Oliver**: Yeah. What makes me so different, anyway? I too have passions, you know.

**Srini**: Oh yes, I do; only too well.

**Oliver**: Yeah. I think the only difference between you guys and me is that I think somewhat differently. Why? I don't know. But my mind, too, romps around the women. What I wonder about all the time is whether our women normally wear panties. I have a sneaking suspicion they don't.

*Ebby colors a little, Abdu looks up in surprise, and Srini almost chokes after a short, quick gulp.*

**Oliver**: Got you, eh? But the truth is ... I really don't know. Because where I belong, they are a must.

See, I told you I think differently.

I also wonder about the particular hue a really dark-complexioned woman wears downstairs. And I often fantasize about platinum blondes.

And because I think quirky, I get round to thinking that women must have their quirky thoughts too. They may not express themselves as openly as we do, but nothing stops the mind from wandering, no?

**Abdu**: Marki! You're really nuts, Oliver.

**Oliver**: Did you know that homely women make the best bed-spreads? The better-looking types don't always go the whole hog because they know that we'll be back, some time or other. But the ordinary variety has to make it magnetic; always.

So, next time you want a jiggle, choose right.

*Oliver pours another round. The men are sweating, even though the fans are on. Abdu's eyes have taken on a glassiness and Ebby's have turned reddish.*

**Srini**: Eat up, Sirs. That will keep the balance.

**Abdu**: Yeah.

*Abdu puts some scramble into his mouth, awkwardly. Ebby gestures to Oliver with the index finger of his left hand. Both of them go through the dining room door, Ebby just a little unsteadily.*

**Abdu** (*in a whisper*): What's happened to Oliver?

**Srini**: Oh, don't mind him, Sir. These remaining days are not going easy for him. And there's a lot of bitterness in him, too.

**Abdu**: About what?

*Oliver returns, sits, and takes another swig.*

**Abdu**: What's happened to Ebby, Oliver?

**Oliver**: Nothing, nothing. He's just taking a leak. That's all. He's OK.

**Abdu**: I must make a trip, too.

**Oliver**: Go ahead, Sir. You know the place.

*Abdu goes through the dining room door. Srini waits for some time before speaking.*

**Srini**: Both the old men are topping, Oliver.

**Oliver**: Yes, I know. But I think they'll hold up. The trouble is that they like booze but they can't indulge themselves because of the taboos.

*Ebby returns. He seems to have washed his face and combed his hair. He looks at his glass, picks it up, but decides against drinking for the time being.*

**Oliver**: Everything OK, Ebby?

**Ebby**: Yes, Yes, I'm fine.

*Junior, Oliver's first son, comes in through the front door, accompanied by a friend.*

**Junior**: Afternoon, Uncles.

**Ebby and Srini**: Good afternoon, Juno. How are you? Who is this? Your friend?

*Abdu returns to the room and is greeted by Junior, while his friend gives Abdu a smile.*

**Junior**: Yes, this is Saleem, my best friend.

**Abdu, Ebby, and Srini**: Hello, Saleem.

**Saleem**: Hello.

**Junior**: C'mon, let's go in.

**Saleem**: 'Bye. Nice meeting you.

*Junior and Saleem go inside. The men take swigs before the conversation picks up again.*

**Abdu**: I say, Oliver. Saleem looks very much like you.

**Oliver**: I'm innocent, if I'm right in guessing your meaning. Some people do bear striking resemblances to others, by the way. And most human beings do have some common ground … in looks, I mean. They could, however, be worlds apart in attitudes. I remember …

### *Flash-back Memory*

    **Vikram**: Come in, Oliver.

    **"Boy" Oliver**: OK.

    *Vikram and "Boy" Oliver walk into a big, sparsely-furnished room, with a dining table and six chairs to one side of it. A swing, suspended from the ceiling, occupies the center of the room. Vikram's mother, seated on one of the chairs, is in conversation with another lady (in sari).*

    **Lady**: They look like twins.

    **Vikram's Mother**: Yes. But he's Vikram's friend. His mother's a teacher.

**Lady**: I thought he was your son.

**Vikram's Mother**: What made you think that?

**Lady**: Just the resemblance.

**"Boy" Oliver**: Good morning.

**Vikram's Mother**: Good morning, Oliver. How is mummy?

**"Boy" Oliver**: She's fine, thank you.

**Vikram**: Let's go inside, Oliver.

*Vikram and Oliver disappear.*

**Oliver**: That happened to me some twenty years ago. I also remember I was happy at the time; the lady had actually seen no difference between Vikram and me. But that was a long time ago.

*Oliver takes another pull at his rum and lights up a cigarette. He looks up at the ceiling, distantly …*

**Oliver**: Yes … a long time ago.

*Deb walks through the front door.*

**Deb**: Hi, Ol. Hi, everyone.

*The men stand up and exchange pleasantries, while Oliver watches, smilingly.*

**Deb**: I saw Junior coming home. He's here, isn't he?

**Oliver**: Yes, he's inside.

**Deb**: Are we ready for lunch, then? Shall I get things organized?

**Oliver**: Ozzie's not come yet, love. And I think we'll have one more round, at least. But you can get things set.

*Deb is hardly through the connecting door when Ozzie rushes in, hot and sweating.*

**Oliver**: Go and wash up, Ozzie. Then you can have your lunch.

**Ozzie**: And Junior?

**Oliver**: He too. You can both sit here and eat. Put on some music; or the TV, if you want that.

*Ozzie goes off inside.*

*Abdu, who has finished his drink, pours another. He looks at Srini and Ebby. Srini takes a quick gulp and passes his glass to Abdu, who refills it. Ebby refuses another round.*

*Junior and his friend come in to the room, and when they reach the front door, Saleem leaves with a general wave. Junior then goes back to the dining room.*

*The men, Ebby excepting, light up cigarettes. All four seem to have reached near- saturation.*

**Oliver**: Bastards!

*Oliver's sudden and unexpected outburst takes the others by surprise.*

**Abdu, Ebby, and Srini**: What?

**Ebby**: Anything wrong, Oliver?

**Oliver**: No, no. Something suddenly flashed across my mind.

**Abdu**: What?

**Oliver**: No, no, forget it.

**Abdu**: No. Tell us. I thought you meant us.

**Oliver**: No, no. Not at all.

**Srini**: Tell us, then.

**Oliver**: Well, OK, if you really want to know. Even now, after such a long time, it makes me see red.

Many, many years ago, when I first came to Madras, I was walking down the road, the road we lived on, with my wife. She was wearing a dress, see? Suddenly a group of urchins started following us, singing that irritating "Missy, Missy" song. I couldn't do a thing. To stop and face them would have meant accepting the difference. Not to stop was humiliating. The other bastards on the road were grinning and clearly enjoying the spectacle. We didn't stop, just got into an auto and escaped. But the whole time, then and after, I kept thinking: "Why can't the bastards leave us alone?" Even now I feel the same way.

God knows they've got their own bloody customs, some of which seem ridiculous to us.

But we don't interfere. We keep quiet about it.

So why can't they simply leave us alone?

*Deb's voice can be heard from the dining room.*

**Deb**: Ol. Lunch is served.

**Oliver**: Yes, love. We're on our way. Just five minutes.

*Oliver takes another pull at his rum, and even though his glass is not empty, he fills it—sparingly, this time.*

**Oliver**: As if that wasn't bad enough, I had yet another nasty experience. She was expecting Junior at the time. Anyone could have seen that she was heavily pregnant. One day, walking down the road again—not the same one, but in the vicinity—a romeo—middle-aged, at that—drew parallel and deliberately nudged her. You know that kind of cheap bastard, don't you? The kind that rushes off with a leer? But the bastard wasn't fast enough. I caught up with the sod and gave him a pasting that he's probably not forgotten to this day. But, surprisingly, no one else joined in. If it had been another woman, the cheap bastard would have been half murdered.

But … OK, let's have lunch. Bring the bottles. We can have one more round at the table.

*The men manage to get up, glasses in hand, Srini with the bottles too.*

*Before the men can pass through the door, Junior and Ozzie come into the living room, plates in their hands.*

# CURTAIN

# ACT TWO

*During the* **Second Act,** *the action takes place in the dining room. It is about the same size as the living room. A door, at the back, leads off to the kitchen behind. The side walls have doors too, giving access to the bedrooms. There are curtains on both doors leading to the wings. Close to the door connecting the dining room to the kitchen is a medium-sized fridge. On the left wall, flanking both sides of the connecting bedroom door are built-up shelves. These contain crockery, an assortment of table-ware, and a large collection of LP gramophone records. Above the door is a flower-shaped, porcelain time-piece. It shows 1.54 p.m.*

*In the middle of the room is a broad, rectangular, wooden dining table, with six chairs that don't match. There is a table-cloth, and the table is set for four, complete with forks, spoons and knives. The tumblers have covers that display crochet work bordered with beads.*

*As Deb and Ruku bring the special dishes in from the kitchen, Abdu, Ebby, and Srini come into the room from the left. Their hands show signs of washing. Oliver is at the door on the right, waiting for them.*

*Oliver takes his place at the head of the table and the others take their seats at random. Oliver notices their discomfiture and deliberately moves his fork, spoon, and knife, to one side. The others do the same, relieved.*

**Oliver**: (*pointing to the cutlery*): Don't worry about these things, Sirs. They're just a formality. I always eat using my fingers. And will always do so—at home at least—wherever I go.

*Oliver serves out the rice and when the bowls are uncovered, the men help themselves. Deb removes the unwanted cutlery and a few of the bowl lids. She starts pouring water into the tumblers.*

**Oliver**: After all, I've got to thank you people for teaching me how to eat biriyani. I don't think it can really be relished if you're not fisting it. So let's do just that. But this is only fried rice, not biriyani.

*The four start eating. Oliver takes a sip of rum. The others notice their empty glasses.*

**Oliver**: I remember being invited to a "homeward"—a party given by the bride's parents, after the wedding. When it came round to dinner time, there was everyone— they were relations on Deb's side—struggling through the biriyani with forks and spoons. I had had my share of booze, so maybe it was that that gave me courage to use my fingers. Believe me, I was the only one in about two hundred guests to do so. I encountered some curious, quizzical looks, but I couldn't be bothered. I just went on with my eating and, true to myself, took a second helping!

But why aren't you drinking? Let's have one more round before we close up, OK?

*All of them drain their glasses and refill according to their inclinations. Oliver seems to be getting more and more communicative.*

*Ruku hovers about the kitchen door.*

*Deb has disappeared.*

**Oliver**: You know, I have always wanted to be true to

myself. I want to be an Indian, but the place doesn't seem to allow that. I have no connection with England, though I can't get rid of it, culturally and otherwise. How am I to blame if some white man fancied some Indian woman many, many generations ago? But the end-result is that I evolved; yet seem to have no real place—home, I mean. I'm like the steam engine: once vital, but now being phased out and scrapped. That's why I named my home "Erehwon".

Soon it will be a different halt, but will there ever be a final end? A homecoming stop?

**Srini**: Maybe that will come soon, Oliver. In the new place, I mean.

**Oliver**: I hope so; but I don't know. I never wanted to leave India. But even you can see that only loads of nothingness stare at me here. OK, I made it; but my children? I hope I will never change my identity, wherever I live. Too many of us have tried that already. Once they're out they say they're Spanish, or Latin-American, or something. But I see nothing to hide. In fact, I'm proud of my mixed descent.

A true Anglo-Indian is an endangered species. According to our Constitution, you can only be born an Anglo-Indian, not made. So we're unique, like some of the few remaining ethnic groups scattered around the world.

But take a look at the peoples of the world now: mostly mixed races and cross-cultures; even multi-culture.

So why aren't we given a decent chance, even in the land of our birth? Maybe because the "purity" card is still in the mind-set; and mind-sets don't change easily.

*Oliver takes a long pull at his rum. The more he drinks, the more fluently he seems to communicate.*

*The men nibble at their food. Oliver eats some and then continues.*

**Oliver**: I've come across so many people who have tried so pathetically to change their spots.

There was this one who came back to India and said he hated the idea of returning to "shit street". Why did he have to come at all?

There was this other one who felt both ashamed and intimidated by a mere film called "Queenie". What if she had seen our desi version, called "Chattakari"?

There was this other who, arriving in his new country, promptly knelt down and kissed the tarmac. This, he probably thought, was the best way to demonstrate his new allegiance. What he didn't think about was that by giving his lips to the ground below him, he was showing his backside to the heavens above.

And there are many more who still talk of England with fondest hope. All bloody fools, I'm sure.

I don't think anyone can forget—never obliterate—his roots. And what they don't realize is that the foulest dung-heap often produces the fairest flowers.

And then, yes, there was this tale told by one of my friends about an uncle of his—a pure Brit—who, during the War, thought he was doing a perfectly wonderful job, even though that only meant being shot out of a cannon in a touring circus. I really admire the guy. He was just a human cannon-ball, and he was happy to be just that.

But we? And me?

*Ruku leaves her post at the kitchen door and walks up to Oliver.*

**Ruku**: Eat first, Bawa. Food getting cold. After lunch, you talk.

*Oliver drains his glass and hands it over to Ruku.*

**Oliver**: Oh, I forgot about you, ma.

*Oliver examines the rum bottle, which is three-quarter through. He then gives it to Ruku.*

**Oliver**: Here, take this, ma.

**Ruku**: T'ank you, Bawa.

**Ebby**: What will she do when you leave, Oliver?

**Ruku**: *(Butting in before Oliver can answer)*: I get 'nother job, Saar. I good cook. Know all English dishes. I bin cookin' forty-fie years now. All in Anglindian 'omes. Ev'ryone like me. But this Bawa *(pointing to Oliver)*, he best. Like my own son. He not like others. Somet'ing diff'rent.

**Oliver**: OK, ma, OK. Enough.

**Ruku**: All right, Bawa. I goin'.

*Ruku shuffles away and the men begin their lunch in earnest.*

*Deb enters through the door on the right, flits about, sees that there is plenty on the table, and disappears into the living room, where the boys are having lunch.*

*The boys come into the dining room and head for the kitchen, empty plates in hand.*

**Abdu**: Junior, Ozzie, come and take some more.

**Ebby**: Yes, come on boys. There's plenty.

**Junior**: No thank you, Uncle.

**Ozzie**: I'm full, Uncle. I don't want.

*The boys pass through the kitchen door.*

# CURTAIN

# ACT THREE

*The living room. The men are seated—lounging, actually—placidly smoking.*

**Abdu**: That was a good meal, Oliver. The drink was equally enjoyable. After a long time, I've really had a good time.

**Srini**: Yeah. Ayah did a splendid job.

**Oliver**: I know. She's good; and faithful.

**Ebby**: So what else is left out, Oliver? You still seem to have a lot of packing to do.

**Oliver**: Not really, Ebby. Most of the stuff has been sold. It'll be collected over the weekend. For the last two days, our friends here will look after us.

**Srini**: Do you need any help? If there's anything, let us know.

**Abdu and Ebby**: Yes.

**Oliver**: I think everything's looked after. But thank you, anyway. If there's anything, I'll get to you.

**Ebby**: By now you must have given all your people a last look-up, eh?

**Oliver**: Yeah, most of them. Staying so far away is a blessing; much more of a blessing than a curse. We don't have too many friends—real friends, I mean. So that part's easy.

We have to go to Shirin's place this evening. You know her—my student, who's engaged to Mahmood, another student of ours? After that visit, no more.

I'll be here, anyway, if anyone wants to see me.

**Ebby**: Have you really thought out your plans and prospects, Oliver?

**Oliver**: Yes, yes, but not too seriously. I want some time to settle down. I definitely want a lot of time for myself. I want space—a lot of it—for mind and body.

**Srini**: You'll surely get a lot over there.

**Oliver**: I hope so. I want to take time off to look at my life. And I want to, if possible, write; put my thoughts and ideas down. I want to follow the strand I picked up in the work of Joyce. I want to write something about the young man as an artist. But here I've never been able to get down to it. I'm already thirty-five. I need to get a move on. I would like, sometime soon, to "forge in the smithy of my soul the uncreated conscience of my race". I don't know if I'm quoting exactly, but that's what I would like to do. I hope it will all come together soon.

**Ebby**: Well, all the best in your endeavors, Oliver. If anyone can do that, it's got to be you.

**Srini**: Yes.

**Oliver**: Well, anyone for anymore? Or are we going to settle for tea?

**Ebby**: Yes, Tea'll be fine. And anyway, we've got a long way to go. I don't think we should have any more.

Why don't we make a promise, however? If you ever return to India, Oliver, we could all get together again. But that treat will be on us, agreed?

**Srini**: Yes, that's a good idea.

**Abdu**: But that won't stop me from having a little something now and again. Yes, let's promise to meet.

**Srini**: OK, on the first Saturday that you're back here, we'll get together and re-live old times. That will be nice. It's sure going to be different when you leave, Oliver.

*Oliver wrings his hands.*

**Oliver**: What's to be done? But this is sure; I'll be there for that party. I don't know when I'll be able to return, but I'll make it.

And anyway, my final resting place is going to be in a small grave in the cemetery beyond the railway lines. It's such a wonderfully peaceful place.

**Abdu**: Come, come; no morbid thoughts, now.

**Oliver**: OK, I've done. The promise is made.

*Abdu looks up at the time-piece. Oliver follows his gaze.*

**Abdu**: Well, it's going to be three. We'd better be going.

**Oliver**: Not before tea. Or would you like coffee?

**Srini**: Tea, just tea.

**Oliver**: OK. (*Calling out to Deb*) Deb, is the tea ready?

**Deb**: (*from well within*) Yes, Ol. Just a minute.

**Ebby**: Well, that's that. Don't forget to keep in touch, Oliver.

**Oliver**: Yeah, sure. You know how it is. But I'll do that, don't worry.

**Srini**: I'll come to the airport.

**Oliver**: If you can. Don't put yourself out.

**Srini**: No, no problem, Oliver.

*Deb comes into the room with the tea-tray. She has changed her outfit, and looks fresh and charming. She goes over to each of the men; then sits next to Oliver.*

**Ebby**: (*to Deb*) So, are you happy?

**Deb**: Yes, excited and a bit afraid. It's all going to be completely new; and sad, of course. This place is our real home. Ol. loves it so much.

**Oliver**: Well, that can't be helped now. The dream's over. It's finished.

**Abdu**: Don't worry, Oliver. Everything will work out for the best.

**Ebby**: Yes.

**Srini**: Sure.

*Deb rises to collect the tea things. When she's done, she takes the tray inside.*

*The men get to their feet and straighten themselves up a bit. Ebby is the first to approach Oliver.*

**Ebby**: 'Bye.

*They shake hands, and then hug each other.*

*Abdu is next; he does the same.*

**Srini**: OK, Oliver, my turn.

**Oliver**: Yeah. 'Bye Srini. Take care.

*Srini and Oliver shake hands, and then clasp each others arms. They drift into a bear-hug, which lingers on.*

*Deb is at the connecting door and her eyes are brimming over.*

**Srini**: 'Bye, Oliver. Be good.

*Oliver struggles to break free and to control himself at the same time.*

*The men pass through the front door, silently.*

*Oliver waits for Deb. Then they follow them to the door.*

**Abdu**: 'Bye. All the best.

**Ebby**: 'Bye. God bless.

**Srini**: See you soon, Oliver. 'Bye.

**Deb**: Thanks for coming. 'Bye.

**Oliver**: 'Bye.

# CURTAIN

# ACT FOUR

**Ten years later.**

*The home of Shirin and Mahmood.*

*The action takes place in the living room. It is spacious, with a huge window on the right, elegantly curtained. On the left is a stair-case to the bedrooms upstairs. Next to the stairs is a door, kept closed. Another door, curtained, shields the view of the dining area.*

*The living room is tastefully bare. One portrait adorns the back wall. A four-seater, leather-upholstered sofa is on the right, with small, ornamental tables on both sides. The set is complete with two armchairs to the back wall, a plush, rectangular, glass-topped table separating them. Up front, facing the armchairs, is a two-seater. A "period" fan, with light fixture, hangs overhead. The floor is carpeted in a suitable shade, the walls ivory.*

*Shirin is talking to her daughters, Farida and Fauzia. She is draped in a flowered, light-colored sari, while the children are in salwar-khameez. They are sitting on the four-seater, with Shirin in the middle.*

**Shirin**: Father has gone to bring that Aunty and Uncle home, dears. They are coming by plane from far away. They are our good friends. They are coming to stay with us for some time. So we must be very good, OK?

*Farida nods her head.*

**Fauzia**: OK … Mummy, will they bring something nice for us?

**Shirin**: Yes, my dear, but you mustn't ask them.

**Farida**: Why didn't we see them before this, mummy?

**Shirin**: They are from another country, Farida.

**Farida**: Then why are they coming here?

**Shirin**: Well, they used to live here in Madras a long time ago. That's when Father and I knew them. That Uncle was my teacher.

**Fauzia**: He teached you when you were small, mummy?

**Shirin** (*laughing*): No, darling, no. I was a big girl then. That Uncle taught me when I was in college.

**Fauzia**: You like him, no, mummy?

**Shirin** (*puzzled*): Er … yes. But they are both our good friends. You like your friends too, don't you?

**Fauzia**: Yes.

**Farida**: How long will they be here, mummy?

**Shirin**: About a month. Maybe less. Why?

**Farida**: Where will they stay?

**Shirin**: Here, of course. They'll be in the spare room.

**Farida**: Why only they two are coming, mummy?

**Shirin**: For a holiday, darling. They too have children; three boys. But the boys aren't coming this time.

**Fauzia**: Is that Aunty pretty, mummy?

**Shirin**: Yes, dear. Why do you ask so many questions?

*Shirin gathers Fauzia into her arms.*

**Fauzia**: I like to be pretty.

**Shirin** (*laughing*): You will be, darling. You already are. And Farida, too.

*Shirin goes to the front door; the girls scamper after her. She sees nothing to interest her, so she turns and goes into the dining room.*

**Fauzia**: Mummy, mummy, I'm hungry. I want to eat.

*Shirin returns, smiling. She looks at Farida.*

**Shirin**: What about you, Fari? Do you want to eat too?

*Farida bobs her head up and down.*

**Shirin**: OK, come on. I'll serve you both. Then you'll be ready when they come. But wait here till I call you. They may come any minute now. And after I serve, you can eat at the table. Not here, OK?

**Farida and Fauzia**: OK, mummy.

*Shirin goes into the dining room. The children stand by the front door and look out eagerly. Their enthusiasm diminishes as time ticks away.*

**Shirin** (*Coming through the connecting door*): Children, come and eat. Breakfast's ready. Be careful not to untidy the place, OK?

*Farida and Fauzia run across the room. Shirin follows them inside. She comes out seconds later, goes to the front door, but sees nothing. She sits down on the two-seater and looks around the room.*

**Shirin**: Farida, Fauzia, remember what you have to say when Aunty and Uncle come?

*They answer from inside.*

**Farida**: Yes, mummy.

**Fauzia**: Good morning, Aunty. Good morning, Uncle. How are you?

**Shirin**: All right. Don't forget.

*A minute later a familiar honk is heard, and Shirin goes to the front door hurriedly. She beams at the party outside.*

**Shirin**: Welcome, welcome.

*Deb walks up to the front door, and the two women embrace. Both seem happy to see each other.*

*Deb hasn't changed much.*

**Shirin**: Come on in. You must be tired.

**Deb**: No, not really. Excited, rather.

*Deb's back is to the dining room, so she doesn't see the girls peeking at her from behind the curtain. Their mouths are somewhat open, in surprise.*

*Mahmood and Oliver come in, each carrying a suitcase. These are deposited by the stairs. Oliver turns to Shirin. He has a generous amount of gray hair now, but otherwise seems the same.*

*Oliver goes up to Shirin, hands outstretched. She takes them in her own, as they look at each other. He moves back and takes a good look.*

**Oliver**: So, Shirin, it's been a long time, eh? But you're looking good.

**Shirin**: Thank you. Both of you are looking well, too. Sit down, sit down, please. Mahmood, you too.

*Deb takes an armchair, while Mahmood walks to the four-seater. Oliver plonks into the double.*

**Oliver**: Wow! It's good to be back. You never know what you're missing until you find that it's no longer there. But homecoming is just great. The place has changed, but the magic is still there.

*Shirin crosses to the dining room door.*

**Shirin**: Well, what would you like? Tea, or coffee?

**Deb**: Coffee, please, Shirin.

**Oliver**: Anything, Shirin. But where are your girls? I'm waiting to see them.

*Farida and Fauzia creep in behind their mother. They look shyly at Deb and Oliver, but say nothing.*

**Shirin**: What must you say to Aunty and Uncle, darlings?

*The girls don't take the hint, so Shirin tries to hide her embarrassment. The girls continue to stare at the guests.*

**Oliver**: Oh, forget all that, Shirin. Hey, Fauzia, come here; see what I've got for you. Come on, come and see.

*Fauzia hesitates, then runs over, and is established on Oliver's knees.*

**Oliver**: You, too, Farida. Come on.

*Farida is more apprehensive, but is pushed forward by her mother. Farida, too, is deposited on Oliver's knees. He draws out some trinkets from his pocket. The girls squeal in delight.*

**Oliver**: Just wait till you see what I really have for you both. But that will have to come a bit later. I'll have to open the cases. Can you wait?

*The girls look at their mother. She smiles, and then goes to the base of the stairs and, looking upwards, calls out.*

**Shirin**: Mary, Mary?

*From above, a friendly voice is heard.*

**Mary**: Coming, Madam.

*Sounds of footsteps are heard on the stairs. Everyone is looking in that direction, as Mary finally comes into sight, halfway down the stairs.*

*Mary is a fair-complexioned, agreeable, well-made woman of forty-five or so. She wears a blue-and-white, polka-dotted, full-skirted, ankle-length dress, and flat-heeled shoes. The apron she wears becomes her.*

*Oliver's face shows some kind of consternation.*

**Mary**: You called, Madam?

# CURTAIN

# ACT FIVE

*The Bar at the **Saverna**, which has served as a rendezvous point for the men for many years, retains its ambience: soft lighting, low tables surrounded by four armchairs, ashtrays, snack bowls and, at the back, the raised bar with its stools, behind which are shelves with an extensive range of liquor on display. A clock in the shelves shows that it is 11.15 in the morning.*

*Abdu, Ebby, and Srini are at a table up front, where they have a good view of the TV. All of them look their ages.*

*Snacks are already on the table, and the ash-tray has begun to fill up. The Manager, now almost a friend, comes up and greets the men with the easy camaraderie that he maintains with the regulars. He is dressed in casuals, but has a look of authority.*

**Manager:** Good morning, Sirs. This is an early surprise. Are we ready to order?

**Abdu:** Good morning, Boss. Yes, it is a bit early, but we arranged for this get-together more than ten years back.

*Abdu looks at Ebby and Srini, and then up at the Manager.*

**Abdu:** We're expecting another friend. He should be here any minute. But there's nothing wrong with getting started. OK, it will be beer for starters. Kingfisher, four bottles, please.

*The Manager summons the Bearer and instructs him. After he goes, the Manager gives the men a "thumbs up", and departs.*

*Oliver strides in just then. He is in jeans, a colorful silk shirt with a distinctive Indian design, and sneakers. He goes up to the men, who stand, ready to greet him. Oliver shakes hands, and hugs each of them, before sitting down.*

*The Bearer appears with four tall tumblers and four bottles of chilled Kingfisher. He looks at Abdu, who gives him the OK. The bearer opens one bottle after the other, and fills each glass to the brim.*

*The four men raise their glasses, and, putting them together with a clink, they toast themselves.*

**All**: Cheers!

**Oliver**: Wow! Only three days since we arrived, but it seems much longer.

**Srini**: That means you must have been busy. Doing what?

**Oliver**: Well, we relaxed on the first day. On the next, we visited Veteran Lines, where we used to live. It's changed a bit, but the old charm is still there.

That night we took the train to Trichy, spent the day with relations and got the night train back to Madras. We reached only this morning. I wasn't going to miss this treat for anything. And, of course, the church services in Pallavaram tomorrow morning.

**Abdu**: I hope you've got the day off. We'll finish off here and go some place else for lunch. And then, we'll take it from there.

**Oliver**: Fine, fine.

**Ebby**: So Oliver, it's been hectic, eh?

**Oliver**: Yes, it has. And it will continue to be, I suppose. We've got such a lot of traveling to do. We want to see as much of the country as we can.

**Abdu**: When you were here, you hardly traveled, Oliver.

**Oliver**: Yes, but that was because there was no money to spare. It's a little different now.

**Srini**: Hope you both enjoy yourselves. But what about Australia? How was it there?

**Oliver**: It's a different world altogether. No one seems to have any time off. Of course, weekends are when people get together, but letting off steam once a week isn't quite life, as I see it. Here we were more relaxed; there, it's nothing but work.

**Ebby**: So you settled down to teaching again, eh?

**Oliver**: I tried my hand at other things, but didn't do too well. I'm good in the classroom, and the pay's good, too. So, yeah, I decided to do what I do best.

*All of them top up their beers, and Abdu summons the Bearer. Oliver goes for a double-large rum-and-coke, while the others settle for whiskey-and-soda. The Bearer takes the order, removes the empty beer bottles, and replaces the ash-tray.*

**Srini**: What about the other stuff?

**Oliver**: What other stuff?

**Srini**: You know, the women.

**Abdu**: Yes, tell us.

**Oliver**: Yeah, there are lots of them ready and willing to be laid, but the encounters were too casual for me.

**Abdu**: What? No commitment and you're not happy? That's just the kind of relationship I'd like to be in.

**Ebby**: But sex for the sake of sex is bestial. Besides, it's demeaning and often dangerous.

**Srini** (*incredulous*): Now you tell me!

**Abdu**: (*to Oliver*): But you did have a go, right?

**Oliver**: Yeah, on the rare occasion. But not any more. Kids growing up and all that kind of thing. Also, the urge isn't really there. So …

*The Bearer puts down the drinks, clears the beer glasses, and replaces the snack bowls.*

**Abdu**: Well, you probably know that this is my last year. I'm superannuated, actually. Just a few months to go.

**Ebby**: It will be my turn next, but that's the way things are.

**Srini** (*to Oliver*): So, what's new here? Has anything changed?

**Oliver**: Yeah, sure. When we reached Shirin's and Mahmood's place, I was shocked to see that they had an Anglo-Indian maid. Only then did I realize why Shirin's little girls hesitated to come to us. What goes around must come around, I'm afraid. But it was a wake-up call, for sure. Things in that sphere of society have certainly changed.

**Abdu**: What else?

**Oliver**: When we visited Veteran Lines, we were very sad to see that so many Anglo-Indians had abandoned the place. It bears the same name, it even has a few old-fashioned but well-maintained bungalows, but the newer ones are a bit too garish. But nothing will alter that, too.

*Oliver polishes off his drink, orders another, and chomps on the snacks that are on the table. All of them are sweating slightly, even though the room is air-conditioned.*

**Abdu**: Where would you like to have lunch, Oliver?

**Oliver**: That's your choice, not mine.

**Abdu**: Ebby, Srini, any ideas?

**Ebby**: Karaikudi's close by, and it has variety. Then there's that Chinese joint in Adyar. Of course, we can go to good old Safari, or even Buhari on Mount Road.

**Srini**: What about Ponnusamy? We could use the AC room. Zumzum is too far off.

**Abdu**: So, Oliver, Karaikudi or Ponnusamy, which?

**Oliver**: Karaikudi. I've never been there. But let's get on with this (*he points to the booze*), for the present.

*All of them drain their glasses, and Abdu orders for refills.*

**Oliver**: It's been great. I wonder if this will ever happen again. I hope it will.

**Srini**: Who knows? We still have this re-union. Let's make the most of it.

**Abdu**: Yes; before I become an elder statesman.

**Ebby**: We'll all have our memories, anyway. Those can never go away. And they can't be taken from us, either.

*As the men continue to indulge their thirst, they unconsciously become silent and reflective. It seems as if a brooding presence comes over them. Srini is the first to break free from the enveloping gloom.*

**Srini**: Come on, I say. Let's drink up and get the hell out of here. It's becoming too dreary. Bottoms up, everybody?

**Abdu, Ebby, and Oliver**: OK!

*The drinks over, the Bearer is summoned and, while the bill goes for payment, Abdu and Srini have a quiet smoke.*

*When the Bearer returns, the four men trudge out.*

*They pass, down the aisle to the main entrance of the auditorium, leaving the audience behind them.*

# CURTAIN